An I Can Read Book™

Amazing TIGERS!

Written by Sarah L. Thomson

Photographs provided by the
Wildlife Conservation Society

HarperCollins*Publishers*

WILDLIFE
CONSERVATION
SOCIETY

Everybody knows

that tigers have stripes.

But did you know

that each tiger's stripes

are different?

If you look carefully, you can see

that no two tigers look the same.

Stripes help tigers hide.

A tiger hides in the grass.

The grass is long and thin.

A tiger has long, thin stripes.

The stripes make the tiger
hard to see.

This is called camouflage.

(Say it like this:

CAM-oh-FLAHG.)

Tigers hide when they hunt.

They hunt deer or wild pigs

or wild cows.

These animals are called prey.

(It sounds the same as PRAY.)

If a hungry tiger

sees or smells a deer,

the tiger does not chase it.

A tiger can run fast,

but a deer can run faster.

A tiger sneaks up on a deer.

It is slow and careful.

It does not make a sound.

If you walked as slowly

as a hunting tiger,

it would take you ten minutes

to get from home plate to first base.

When a tiger is close enough,

it jumps on its prey!

Hunting is hard work.

A tiger might try ten times,

or even twenty,

before it catches a meal.

All cats are hunters, just like tigers.

House cats are pets.

Other cats, like lions and tigers, are wild.

Tigers are the biggest cats of all.

A big tiger can weigh 550 pounds.

That's more than

two baby elephants.

Young tigers are called cubs.
They are much smaller
than grown-up tigers.
Tiger cubs weigh only
two or three pounds
when they are born.
Human babies weigh
about eight pounds
when they are born.

A mother tiger has

two or three or four cubs.

She takes care of them by herself.

The father tiger does not stay

with the mother and cubs.

Cubs learn by watching their mother.

They learn to hunt.

They learn to find water

for drinking and swimming.

Most cats do not like to swim.

But tigers do.

The place where a tiger lives

is called its territory.

No other tiger lives there.

Tigers rub against trees and rocks

to leave behind their smell.

They stand on their back legs

and use their claws

to make long scratches in tree bark.

These are signs.

They tell other tigers, "Stay out!"

Tigers can live in forests
or jungles or swamps.
Some live in Russia,
where it is cold and snowy
in the winter.

Some live in parts of India,

where it is hot almost all the time.

There may be fewer than ten thousand

tigers left in the wild.

A hundred years ago

here were about a hundred thousand.

What happened to all the tigers?

People chop down the forests

where tigers live.

They plant crops,

or build houses,

or sell the trees for wood.

Then tigers have nowhere to live.

The animals they hunt

have nowhere to live.

Tigers hunt animals to eat.

But someone hunts tigers—
people.

People hunt tigers

for their striped skins

to make into clothes or rugs.

Some people think
a tiger's bones and whiskers
can make sick people well.
It is against the law to kill tigers.
But some people break the law.

Scientists study tigers
so people can help them.
Tigers hunt at night
and sleep during the day.
They hide from people.
To find tigers,
scientists set up a camera
in the forest.

When a tiger walks by,

the camera takes its picture.

Since each tiger's stripes

are different,

scientists can use these pictures

to count how many tigers there are.

Other times scientists shoot a tiger

with a dart that puts it to sleep.

This does not hurt the tiger.

When it wakes up,

it is wearing a collar.

The collar sends out radio signals.

The signals tell the scientists

where the tiger goes.

When we know
how many tigers there are,
and where they are,
then we will have a better idea
how to help them.

People have made it hard

for tigers to live.

Now people must help tigers.

People can stop cutting down forests.

We can stop buying tiger skins

and medicines that are made

from tigers' bodies.

We can make parks

where no one is allowed to hunt.

Tigers can live there and be safe.

If we do all these things,

then maybe, a hundred years from now,

there will be

a hundred thousand tigers again.

The Wildlife Conservation Society and Tigers

The Wildlife Conservation Society (WCS) saves wildlife and wild lands around the world, studies and teaches about what animals need to survive, and runs the world's largest system of zoos, including the Bronx Zoo in New York City. The WCS Tiger Program works to save tigers and bring them back to the places where they once lived. Years ago tigers could be found across all of Asia. Now there may be fewer than 10,000 tigers in the wild. The WCS goal is for there to be 100,000 wild tigers in 100 years.

WCS scientists spend time in Asia studying the size and location of tiger populations. When scientists discover large numbers of tigers, organizations like WCS can work to protect them and their homes. WCS also teaches people about the dangers tigers face, especially from illegal hunting, and helps many countries create parks where tigers can be protected.

Six Siberian, or Amur, tigers—Norma, Sasha, Alexis, Lantar, Taurus, and Zeff—live in Tiger Mountain, a new exhibit at the Bronx Zoo. Here people can see tigers up close and learn about what can be done to save them. To find out more about WCS and the ways you can help tigers and other endangered animals, visit WCS online at www.wcs.org.

With gratitude to Peter Hamilton. Also special thanks for photographs to Dennis DeMello (jacket front and back, front flap, pages 2, 3, 6-7, 8-9, 10, 12, 14, 17, 24-25, 29, 31, 32), John Goodrich (title page), and Ullas Karanth (pages 4-5, 23, 26, 27, 28), as well as Praveen Bhargav (page 11 lower), Maurice Hornocker (pages 16, 18), Diane Shapiro (pages 11 upper, 20), and Diane Waller (pages 15, 21).

Library of Congress Cataloging-in-Publication Data
Thomson, Sarah L.   Amazing tigers! / Sarah L. Thomson ; photographs provided by the Wildlife Conservation Society.— 1st ed.   cm. (An I can read book)   Summary: Discusses the physical characteristics, behavior, habitat, life cycle, and endangered status of tigers.   ISBN 0-06-054450-3 — ISBN 0-06-054451-1 (lib. bdg.) — ISBN 0-06-054452-X (pbk.)
1. Tigers—Juvenile literature. [1. Tigers.   2. Endangered species.] I. Wildlife Conservation Society (New York, N.Y.) II. Title.   III. Series.   QL737.C23T47373 2004   599.756—dc22
2003017692